Cheerios®
Cookbook

Tasty Treats and Clever Crafts for Kids

WILEY

...ley Publishing, Inc.

For general information on our other products and services or to obtain technical support please contact our Customer Care Department within U.S. at (800) 762-2974, outside the U.S. at (317) 572-3993 or fax (317) 572-4002.

Wiley also publishes its books in a variety of electronic formats. Some content that appears in print may not be available in electronic books.

Library of Congress Cataloging-in-Publication Data:
The Cheerios cookbook : tasty treats and clever crafts for kids.—1st ed.
    p. cm.
    Includes index.
    ISBN-13: 978-0-7645-9609-4 (hardcover : alk. paper)
    ISBN-10: 0-7645-9609-8 (hardcover : alk. paper)
 1. Cookery (Cereals) 2. Cereals, Prepared.
    TX808.C44 2005
    641.6'31—dc22   2005008242

General Mills

Director, Book and Online Publishing:
Kim Walter

Manager, Cookbook Publishing:
Lois Tlusty

Editor: Heidi Losleben

Recipe Development and Testing:
Betty Crocker Kitchens

Photography and Food Styling:
General Mills Photography Studios

Wiley Publishing, Inc.

Publisher: Natalie Chapman

Executive Editor: Anne Ficklen

Editor: Kristi Hart

Production Editor: Paul Sobel

Cover Design: Paul Dinovo

Interior Design and Layout: Fritz Metsch

Photography Art Direction:
Pam Kurtz/Ellen Blasena & Associates

Manufacturing Manager: Kevin Watt

Cover Photos: Ollie Octopus (paage 56) and Frozen Yogonanas (page 59)

For more great ideas visit Cheerios.com

Manufactured in China

10 9 8 7 6 5 4 3 2 1

First Edition

Cover illustrations: Paul Dinovo

Hey Moms (and Anyone Else Who Loves Kids)!

Cooking and eating with your family and friends is a wonderful way to show you care, as is spending time with them in the kitchen. Add some Cheerios cereal, marshmallows or chocolate to the mix, and you've got a time-tested recipe for fun!

The sweet treats, simple snacks and creative crafts that follow were created to nourish and nurture—whether it be a child, grandchild, niece, nephew or next-door neighbor. After all, who better to make memories than Cheerios cereal, a toddler's first finger food?

Hey Kids!

If you love Cheerios cereal, and chances are you do or you wouldn't be looking at this book, you already know it tastes yummy and is good for you. But did you know there's a lot more to Cheerios cereal than meets the breakfast bowl? You can use the cereal as a topping for smoothies, as an ingredient in muffins and cookies, and even to make stuff like a paper-plate starfish or funny foam sunglasses.

So, come on, let's get cooking!

Heidi Losleben,
Editor

Contents

Nurturing through Nutrition

Whether out of the box or in a recipe, everybody loves the toasty oat taste of Cheerios cereal. There are lots of reasons Cheerios cereal is a family favorite: The little round O's are wholesome, versatile and just plain fun to eat!

More Fun Facts about Cheerios Cereal

- Four out of five pediatricians, who recommend finger food for toddlers, recommend Cheerios cereal.

- Cheerios cereal has only 1 gram of sugar per cup (some cereals have more than 10!).

- Cheerios cereal provides 14 essential vitamins and minerals, including Vitamins A, B6, B12, C and D, calcium, iron and folic acid, just to name a few.

- It's all real: There are no artificial colors or flavors in Cheerios cereal.

- Cheerios cereal is made with whole grain oats and is a good source of fiber.

- Cheerios cereal helps develop motor skills because the O's are easy to pick up, are firm, and they resist crumbling.

Recipe for Safety

Although this cookbook is meant for kids, it's no substitute for adult supervision in the kitchen. When it comes to deciding who does what, you are the best judge of your child's skill level and abilities. The recipes were chosen with the idea that a child could lend a hand in at least one of the steps. The most important ingredient in keeping the kitchen a fun, safe place is a caring, watchful adult. You probably already have a good handle on safety, but here are a few gentle reminders.

- Keep emergency phone numbers near the phone and explain to your child when and how to use them.

- Always have a fire extinguisher handy.

- Never leave your child alone in the kitchen.

- Place pans on back burners and turn pot handles toward the back of the stove.

- Both you and your child should wear close-fitting clothing when cooking.

- Make sure hot foods and liquids are out of your child's reach.

- Don't leave cooking food unattended. It is the number one cause of house fires.

- Unplug the cords of appliances and keep them out of your child's reach.

Cooking Checklist

Hey kids! Cooking is fun and you probably can't wait to get started. But before you do, it's a good idea to follow a few guidelines so everything goes smoothly. The most important thing to remember: Always ask a grown-up to help you in the kitchen. Here's a handy checklist to get you started.

Checklist

☑ **1.** I picked out a recipe I want to make.

☐ **2.** I have someone to help me in the kitchen.

☐ **3.** My helper read me the recipe and I understand it.

☐ **4.** I am wearing clothes it's okay to cook in.

☐ **5.** My hair is tied back or out of the way.

☐ **6.** I washed my hands.

☐ **7.** I have all the ingredients I need.

☐ **8.** I have the pots, pans, measuring cups and spoons I need.

☐ **9.** I know what parts of the recipe I can do myself.

Whatchamacallits & Thingamajigs

Do you know the difference between a muffin pan and a measuring spoon? How about a saucepan or a rubber spatula? Have a grown-up read the words on the left and see if you can match them with the right picture.

Rolling Pin

Rubber Spatula

Muffin Pan

Pan (13 x 9-inch)

Electric Mixer

Saucepan

Wire Whisk

Cookie Sheet

My Recipe Diary

Here's a neat place to keep track of the recipes you make. That way you can decide if you would make the recipe again or do something different the next time.

Recipe	Date Made	Person Who Helped Me	Comments	Rate the Recipe*

 = Super Good

= Good

 = Okay

= Yuck

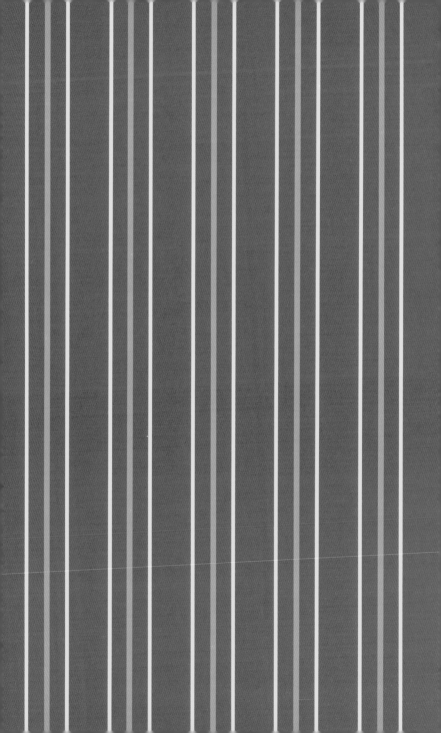

Crush 'em

Very Berry Parfaits

Start to Finish: 10 minutes
2 parfaits

1 cup Berry Burst
Cheerios® cereal (any
flavor)

1/2 cup blueberries,
raspberries or sliced
strawberries

1 container (6 oz) yogurt
(any berry flavor)

1. Pour the cereal into a plastic bag and seal. Slightly crush the cereal with a rolling pin or a can of soup.

2. In 2 (about 1-cup) parfait or drinking glasses, layer half of the berries and half of the yogurt. Top each parfait with half of the crushed cereal.

1 Parfait: Calories 170; Total Fat 2g; Sodium 140mg; Total Carbohydrate 33g (Sugars 22g); Protein 5g • **Exchanges:** 1 1/2 Starch, 1/2 Fruit • **Carbohydrate Choices:** 2

Berry Good

Not only are these parfaits "berry-licious," they are also "berry" healthy. Blueberries provide antioxidants, which are believed to reduce the risk of cancer and heart disease.

Teds on Sleds

2 cups milk

1 box (4-serving size) chocolate or vanilla instant pudding and pie filling mix

2 cups Frosted Cheerios® cereal

1 bar (1.4 to 1.55 oz) milk chocolate or white chocolate candy

Teddy bear shaped graham snacks

1. Pour the milk into a medium bowl. Add the pudding mix. Beat with a wire whisk or rotary beater for 1 to 2 minutes until the pudding is well blended. Divide the pudding evenly into 4 dessert dishes. Let the pudding set for at least 5 minutes.

2. Just before serving, pour the cereal into a plastic bag and seal. Crush the cereal with a rolling pin or a can of soup. Chop the candy. Sprinkle the crushed cereal and chopped candy equally over each dish of pudding. Top each serving with 1 or 2 teddy bear–shaped grahams.

1 Serving: Calories 270; Total Fat 7g; Sodium 520mg; Total Carbohydrate 47g (Sugars 35g); Protein 6g • **Exchanges:** 1 Starch, 2 Other Carbohydrate, 1 1/2 Fat • **Carbohydrate Choices:** 3

Mountain Climbing

Instead of the candy topping, stick a few animal crackers on the pudding as if they're climbing the "mountain."

Twice As Nice

Some starfish can split their bodies in half and grow new legs to make two new starfish.

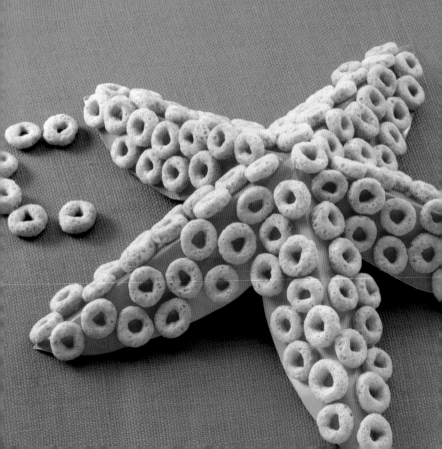

Silly Starfish

Start to Finish: 20 minutes
1 starfish

Pencil

Colorful paper plate

Scissors

Glue

Cheerios cereal

Draw a starfish shape on the paper plate. Cut out the shape.

Fold each leg in half, starting at the tip and moving toward the center.

Make a crease between each leg, folding in the opposite direction, to the center to create a 3-D starfish.

Spread glue all over the starfish and cover with the cereal. Let stand until dry.

Bee's Knees Banana Muffins

Start to Finish: 40 minutes
6 muffins

STREUSEL

1/4 cup Honey Nut Cheerios® cereal

2 teaspoons all-purpose flour

2 teaspoons packed light brown sugar

2 teaspoons butter or margarine, softened

MUFFINS

1 1/2 cups Honey Nut Cheerios cereal

1 pouch (6.4 oz) banana nut muffin mix

1/2 cup milk

1 tablespoon vegetable oil

1 egg

1. Heat the oven to 400°F. Line 6 regular-size muffin cups with paper baking cups or spray just the bottoms of the muffin cups with cooking spray.

2. For the Streusel, pour the 1/4 cup of cereal into a plastic bag and seal. Slightly crush the cereal with a rolling pin or a can of soup. Pour the crushed cereal into a small bowl. Stir in the flour, brown sugar and butter until crumbly. Set the bowl aside.

3. For the Muffins, pour the 1 1/2 cups of cereal into a plastic bag and seal. Slightly crush the cereal with a rolling pin or a can of soup. Pour the muffin mix, milk and oil into a medium bowl. Stir in the egg just until moistened (the batter will be lumpy). Stir in the crushed cereal. Spoon the batter evenly into the muffin cups, filling each to the top. Sprinkle the Streusel evenly over the tops.

4. Bake 15 to 20 minutes or until the muffins are golden brown and the tops spring back when touched lightly. Immediately remove the muffins from the cups. Cool 5 minutes before serving.

1 Muffin: Calories 220; Total Fat 9g; Sodium 310mg; Total Carbohydrate 31g (Sugars 15g); Protein 5g • **Exchanges:** 1 Starch, 1 Other Carbohydrate, 2 Fat • **Carbohydrate Choices:** 2

Muffin Method

Unlike most muffin mixes, which tell you to fill the muffin cups 2/3 full, it's important to fill the cups in this recipe to the top. If you don't, you'll wind up with midget muffins!

Choco Chip Mega Muffins

Start to Finish: 45 minutes
12 muffins

2 cups Cheerios cereal

1 1/4 cups all-purpose flour

1/3 cup packed light brown sugar

1 teaspoon ground cinnamon

1 teaspoon baking powder

3/4 teaspoon baking soda

1 cup applesauce

1/3 cup milk

3 tablespoons vegetable oil

1 egg

1/2 cup miniature chocolate chips

1. Heat the oven to 400°F. Line 12 regular-size muffin cups with paper baking cups or spray just the bottoms of the muffin cups with cooking spray.

2. Pour the cereal into a plastic bag and seal. Crush the cereal with a rolling pin or a can of soup. Pour the crushed cereal into a large bowl. Stir in the flour, brown sugar, cinnamon, baking powder and baking soda. Stir in the rest of the ingredients just until moistened. Spoon the batter evenly into the muffin cups.

3. Bake 18 to 22 minutes or until the muffins are golden brown. Immediately remove the muffins from the cups. Cool 5 minutes before serving.

1 Muffin: Calories 180; Total Fat 7g; Sodium 180mg; Total Carbohydrate 29g (Sugars 14g); Protein 3g • **Exchanges:** 1 Starch, 1 Other Carbohydrate, 1 Fat • **Carbohydrate Choices:** 2

Muffin Music

Need some background music? Sing "The Muffin Man" along with your child as you create these yummy masterpieces.

Crayons were introduced in 1903. The first box of crayons had only eight colors!

Flower Power Crayon Holder

Start to Finish: 20 minutes
1 crayon holder

Scissors	Green pipe cleaners
Blue construction paper	Small colorful pom-poms
Clean, empty soup can	Cheerios cereal
Glue	
Green construction paper	

1. Cut the blue paper to cover the outside of the soup can. Attach it with glue.

2. Cut the green construction paper to look like grass. Glue it to the bottom of the blue paper around the can.

3. Cut the pipe cleaners to make flower stems. Attach them to the can with glue. Glue 1 pom-pom at the top of each stem to make the center of a flower. Glue cereal around the pom-pom to make flower petals.

Apple-Cinnamon Pile o' Pancakes

Start to Finish: 20 minutes
5 servings (2 pancakes and 2 tablespoons syrup each)

1 cup Apple Cinnamon Cheerios® cereal

3/4 cup all-purpose flour

3/4 cup milk

2/3 cup chunky apple-sauce

3 tablespoons butter or margarine, melted

2 teaspoons baking powder

1/4 teaspoon salt

1 egg

Maple-flavored syrup

1. Heat a griddle or a 12-inch skillet over medium-low heat or to 325°F.

2. Pour the cereal into a plastic bag and seal. Crush the cereal with a rolling pin or a can of soup. Pour the crushed cereal into a large bowl. Stir in the rest of the ingredients except the syrup just until moistened.

3. Pour the batter, a generous 1/4 cup at a time, onto the hot griddle. Cook 2 minutes or until the edges look cooked and the bubbles begin to break on the surface. Flip the pancakes and cook the other side until golden brown, about 2 minutes longer. Serve the pancakes with syrup.

1 Serving: Calories 340; Total Fat 9g; Sodium 470mg; Total Carbohydrate 60g (Sugars 26g); Protein 5g • **Exchanges:** 2 Starch, 2 Other Carbohydrate, 1 1/2 Fat • **Carbohydrate Choices:** 4

Tasty Topping

Skip the syrup, and top these moist pancakes with warm apple pie filling or a sprinkle of brown sugar instead.

Press 'em

Marshmallow Melties

Start to Finish: 30 minutes
24 bars

3 tablespoons butter or margarine

1 bag (10.5 oz) miniature marshmallows (6 cups)

5 cups Cheerios cereal

1. Spray the bottom and the sides of a 13 x 9-inch pan with cooking spray.

2. Place the butter and marshmallows in a large microwavable bowl. Microwave uncovered on High for about 2 minutes, stirring after each minute, until the mixture is smooth. With pot holders, remove the bowl from the microwave.

3. Immediately stir in the cereal until it is evenly coated. Pour the cereal mixture into the pan. With the buttered back of a spoon, press the mixture in the pan until it is even. Cool at least 10 minutes.

4. With a table knife, cut the cereal mixture into 6 rows by 4 rows to make 24 bars. Store the bars in a loosely covered container.

1 Bar: Calories 80; Total Fat 2g; Sodium 70mg; Total Carbohydrate 15g (Sugars 7g); Protein 0g
• **Exchanges:** 1/2 Starch, 1/2 Other Carbohydrate, 1/2 Fat • **Carbohydrate Choices:** 1

Count 'em Out

Pour a bunch of marshmallows on the table or counter and have your child figure out how many fit in 1 cup.

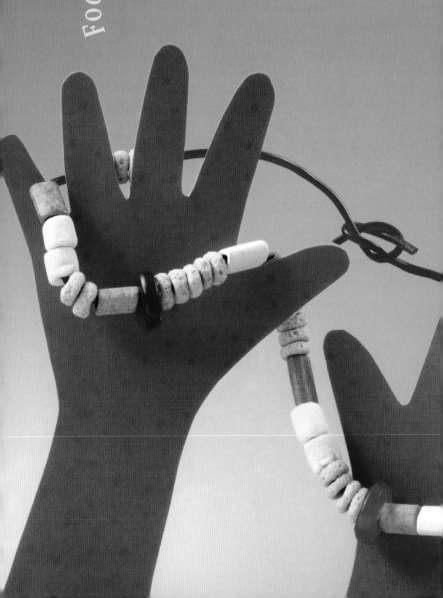

Food by the Foot

A single Cheerios "O" measures about 1/2 inch across, so it takes about 24 O's to make a foot.

String 'n Eat Necklaces

Start to Finish: 45 minutes
4 necklaces

1/3 up Cheerios cereal

1 roll (1.5 oz) brightly colored, ring-shaped gummy candy

1 package (1 1/4 oz) pastel-colored tube-shaped licorice candies

1/2 cup colored miniature marshmallows

4 pieces (about 36 inches each) red shoestring licorice

1 tablespoon all-purpose flour

1. String an arrangement of the cereal, candies and marshmallows onto each piece of shoestring licorice (to prevent stickiness, dip 1 end of the licorice into the flour before poking it through each marshmallow).

2. When each licorice is 3/4 full, tie the ends of the licorice together into a double knot to make a necklace. If desired, wrap plastic wrap around each necklace to keep it clean.

1 Necklace: Calories 180; Total Fat 0.5g; Sodium 105mg; Total Carbohydrate 41g (Sugars 24g); Protein 1g • **Exchanges:** 1 Starch, 1 1/2 Other Carbohydrate • **Carbohydrate Choices:** 3

Caramel Crispies

Start to Finish: 1 hour 20 minutes
36 bars

6 cups Honey Nut Cheerios cereal

1 bag (14 oz) vanilla caramels, unwrapped

3 tablespoons water

2 cups miniature marshmallows

1/2 cup semisweet or milk chocolate chocolate chips

1 tablespoon shortening

1/4 cup miniature candy-coated semisweet chocolate baking bits

1. Spray the bottom and the sides of a 13 x 9-inch pan with cooking spray.

2. Pour the cereal into a large bowl. Set the bowl aside.

3. Place the unwrapped caramels and water in a medium microwavable bowl. Microwave uncovered on High for 2 1/2 to 4 minutes, stirring after each minute, until the mixture is smooth. With pot holders, remove the bowl from the microwave.

4. Pour the caramel mixture over the cereal and stir until the cereal is evenly coated. Gently stir in the marshmallows. Pour the cereal mixture into the pan. With the buttered back of a spoon, press the mixture in the pan until it is even.

5. Place the chocolate chips and shortening in a small microwavable bowl. Microwave uncovered on High for 1 to 2 minutes, stirring after each minute, until the mixture is smooth. Drizzle the chocolate over the top of the cereal mixture. Sprinkle the baking bits evenly over the chocolate. Refrigerate until the mixture is firm and the glaze is set, about 1 hour.

6. With a table knife, cut the cereal mixture into 9 rows by 4 rows to make 36 bars. Store the bars in a loosely covered container.

1 Bar: Calories 90; Total Fat 2.5g; Sodium 75mg; Total Carbohydrate 17g (Sugars 11g); Protein 1g • **Exchanges:** 1/2 Starch, 1/2 Other Carbohydrate, 1/2 Fat • **Carbohydrate Choices:** 1

PB-Chocolate Bars on Cars

Start to Finish: 1 hour 20 minutes
36 bars

6 cups Honey Nut Cheerios cereal

1 1/2 cups miniature marshmallows

1 1/2 cups peanut butter chips

3/4 cup light corn syrup

3 tablespoons butter or margarine

1 cup milk chocolate chips, melted

1. Spray the bottom and the sides of a 13 x 9-inch pan with cooking spray.

2. Pour the cereal and marshmallows into a large bowl. Stir to mix. Set the bowl aside.

3. Place the peanut butter chips and corn syrup in a medium microwavable bowl. Add the butter. Microwave uncovered on High for

2 to 3 minutes, stirring after each minute, until the mixture is smooth. With pot holders, remove the bowl from the microwave.

4. Pour the peanut butter mixture over the cereal mixture and stir until the cereal is evenly coated. Pour the cereal mixture into the pan. With the buttered back of a spoon, press the mixture in the pan until it is even. Spread the melted chocolate evenly over the top. Refrigerate until firm, about 1 hour.

5. With a table knife, cut the cereal mixture into 9 rows by 4 rows to make 36 bars. Store the bars in a loosely covered container.

1 Bar: Calories 120; Total Fat 4.5g; Sodium 85mg; Total Carbohydrate 18g (Sugars 12g); Protein 2g • **Exchanges:** 1/2 Starch, 1/2 Other Carbohydrate, 1 Fat • **Carbohydrate Choices:** 1

On the Stove

You can also use a stove rather than a microwave to create these delicious bars. Make the recipe as directed—except heat the peanut butter chips, corn syrup and butter in a 2-quart saucepan over low heat, stirring constantly, until smooth.

You could also decorate a pair of store-bought plastic sunglasses instead of cutting out your own.

Superhero Shades

Start to Finish: 20 minutes
1 pair of shades

Ruler	Paper hole punch
Pencil	2 pipe cleaners
1 sheet of craft foam (12 x 8 1/2 inch)	Glue
	Cheerios cereal
Scissors	

1. Measure from the center of one of your child's eyes to the center of the other eye with the ruler. Use this measurement to make 2 dots with the pencil in the center of the craft foam the same distance apart as your child's eyes.

2. Draw a 3 1/2-inch shape around each dot for the frames of the glasses. Draw a 1 1/2-inch circle inside each shape for the eye holes. Draw a 1/2-inch-wide strip connecting the 2 shapes. Cut out the frames of the glasses along the lines.

3. Punch holes on either side of the frames with the hole punch. Twist a pipe cleaner onto each hole to create earpieces for the shades.

4. Spread glue on the front of the frames and decorate with the cereal. Let stand until dry.

Honey Nut Stacks of Snacks

Start to Finish: 1 hour 15 minutes
36 bars

1 1/2 cups packed light brown sugar

1 cup butter or margarine

2 cups Honey Nut Cheerios cereal

2 cups quick-cooking or old-fashioned oats

2 teaspoons baking powder

1/2 teaspoon ground cinnamon

1/4 teaspoon salt

1. Heat the oven to 350°F. Place the brown sugar and butter in a 2-quart saucepan. Heat over medium heat, stirring constantly, until smooth. Remove the saucepan from the heat.

2. Stir in the rest of the ingredients. Pour the mixture into an ungreased 13 x 9-inch pan. With a rubber spatula, spread the mixture in the pan until it is even.

3. Bake 16 to 18 minutes or until the edges are golden brown and firm. Place the pan on a wire rack. Cool completely, about 45 minutes.

4. With a table knife, cut the baked mixture into 6 rows by 6 rows to make 36 bars. Store the bars in a loosely covered container.

1 Bar: Calories 110; Total Fat 5g; Sodium 95mg; Total Carbohydrate 13g (Sugars 9g); Protein 0g
• **Exchanges:** 1/2 Starch, 1/2 Other Carbohydrate, 1 Fat • **Carbohydrate Choices:** 1

Quick-Cooking versus Old-Fashioned

Both quick-cooking and old-fashioned oats are rolled oats. The only difference between the two is that the quick oats are cut into lots of pieces before they are steamed and rolled.

PB & J Squares

Start to Finish: 1 hour 20 minutes
24 bars

6 cups Cheerios cereal

1/2 cup peanuts

1/2 cup raisins

1/3 cup grape jelly

1/4 cup sugar

1/4 cup light corn syrup

1/2 cup creamy peanut
butter

1. Spray the bottom and the sides of a 13 x 9-inch pan with cooking spray.

2. Pour the cereal, peanuts and raisins into a large bowl. Stir to mix. Set the bowl aside.

3. Place the jelly, sugar and corn syrup in a 2-quart saucepan. Heat over medium heat, stirring occasionally, until the mixture starts to boil. Boil for 2 minutes, stirring frequently. Remove the saucepan from the heat. Stir in the peanut butter until the mixture is smooth.

4. Pour the peanut butter mixture over the cereal mixture and stir until everything is evenly coated. Pour the mixture into the pan. With the buttered back of a spoon, press the mixture in the pan until it is even. Cool completely, about 1 hour.

5. With a table knife, cut the cereal mixture into 6 rows by 4 rows to make 24 bars. Store the bars in a loosely covered container.

1 Bar: Calories 120; Total Fat 4.5g; Sodium 110mg; Total Carbohydrate 17g (Sugars 8g); Protein 3g • **Exchanges:** 1/2 Starch, 1/2 Other Carbohydrate, 1 Fat • **Carbohydrate Choices:** 1

Bowl of Fun

Have your child mix up the cereal, peanuts and raisins in the large bowl (Step 2). Provided the bowl is deep enough, spillage shouldn't be a problem.

Roll 'em

O My! Giant Oat Cookies

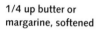

Start to Finish: 1 hour
12 large cookies

1/4 up butter or
margarine, softened

1 1/2 cups sugar

1/3 cup vegetable oil

1 teaspoon vanilla

2 eggs

1 1/2 cups all-purpose
flour

1 cup quick-cooking or
old-fashioned oats

1 teaspoon baking soda

1/2 teaspoon salt

3 cups Cheerios cereal

1. Heat the oven to 375°F. Place the butter and sugar in a large bowl. Beat with an electric mixer on medium speed until blended. Beat in the oil, vanilla and eggs until well combined. On low speed, beat in the flour, oats, baking soda and salt until a dough forms. With a spoon, stir in the cereal.

2. For each cookie, roll 1/3 cup of the dough into a ball. Place the balls 2 inches apart onto 2 ungreased cookie sheets.

3. Bake 9 to 11 minutes or until the cookies are light brown. Cool the cookies for 2 minutes on the cookie sheets. Then, remove them from the cookie sheets and place on wire racks. Cool completely, about 20 minutes. Store the cookies in a tightly covered container.

1 Large Cookie: Calories 310; Total Fat 12g; Sodium 310mg; Total Carbohydrate 47g (Sugars 26g); Protein 5g • **Exchanges:** 1 1/2 Starch, 1 1/2 Other Carbohydrate, 2 Fat • **Carbohydrate Choices:** 3

Cookie Crumbles

Even though it may be difficult, it's important to let these cookies cool a few minutes before removing them from the cookie sheets. Otherwise they may break into pieces.

Snacks on Sticks

Start to Finish: 50 minutes
10 snacks

1/4 cup butter or margarine

3 cups miniature marshmallows

1/4 cup creamy peanut butter

4 cups Cheerios cereal

1/2 cup raisins

1/3 cup sunflower nuts

10 flat wooden sticks with round ends

1. Place a sheet of waxed paper on the kitchen counter.

2. Place the butter and marshmallows in a 3-quart saucepan. Heat over low heat, stirring constantly, until the mixture is smooth. Stir in the peanut butter until the mixture is well blended. Remove the saucepan from the heat.

3. Stir in the cereal, raisins and sunflower nuts until everything is evenly coated. Cool for 2 minutes.

4. Lightly spray your hands with cooking spray. Shape the mixture into 10 (2-inch) balls. Insert 1 wooden stick into the center of each ball. Place the snacks on the waxed paper. Cool completely, about 30 minutes. Store in a loosely covered container.

1 Snack: Calories 230; Total Fat 11g; Sodium 200mg; Total Carbohydrate 29g (Sugars 14g); Protein 4g • **Exchanges:** 1 Starch, 1 Other Carbohydrate, 2 Fat • **Carbohydrate Choices:** 2

Cool and Colorful

These tasty snacks are even more fun if you wrap them in colored plastic wrap after they cool.

Shape Up

Instead of a heart, try making a square-, a circle- or a triangle-shaped frame.

I "Heart" You Picture Frame

Start to Finish: 30 minutes
1 picture frame

Photo	Scissors
File folder (any color) or lightweight cardboard	Glue
	Cheerios cereal
Pencil	Decorating spray for cakes

1. Place the photo on the file folder, keeping the folder folded so you have 2 layers. Lightly outline the edge of the photo with the pencil. Set aside the photo. Draw a heart shape about 1 inch larger than the photo outline. Cut the heart shape out of the doubled folder. You'll wind up with 2 hearts.

2. At the bottom of 1 heart, make 2 (1-inch) cuts, 1 inch apart, on either side of the heart's point. Fold this piece back to make a stand on the back of the frame.

3. Cut out the center of the remaining heart to within about 1 inch of the edges. Place this heart over the photo. Use it as a guide to trim the photo to fit. Set the photo aside.

4. Glue the bottom and side edges of the 2 hearts together, leaving an opening in the top large enough to slip the photo into the frame. Glue cereal over the front of the frame. Let stand until dry.

5. Spray the cereal with the decorating spray, if desired. Let stand until the spray is dry. Insert the photo into the frame.

Snowball Surprises

Start to Finish: 50 minutes
20 snacks

1/3 cup sugar

1/2 cup light corn syrup

1/2 cup creamy or crunchy peanut butter

3 cups Frosted Cheerios cereal

1 to 2 tablespoons candy sprinkles

20 small candies

1. Line a cookie sheet with waxed paper.

2. Pour the sugar and corn syrup into a 3-quart saucepan. Heat over medium heat, stirring frequently, just until the mixture starts to boil. Remove the saucepan from the heat. Stir in the peanut butter until the mixture is well blended.

3. Stir in the cereal until it is evenly coated. Cool for 5 minutes. While the mixture is cooling, place the candy sprinkles in a shallow dish.

4. Lightly spray your hands with cooking spray. For each snack, shape about 1/4 cup of the cereal mixture into a ball around 1 small candy. Immediately roll the ball in the candy sprinkles to coat. Place the balls on the cookie sheet. Cool completely, about 30 minutes. Store the snacks in a loosely covered container.

1 Snack: Calories 120; Total Fat 3.5g; Sodium 75mg; Total Carbohydrate 21g (Sugars 15g); Protein 2g • **Exchanges:** 1/2 Starch, 1 Other Carbohydrate, 1/2 Fat • **Carbohydrate Choices:** 1 1/2

I Want Candy

Need candy ideas? Try using miniature milk chocolate candy drops or pieces, small gumdrops, chocolate-covered raisins, miniature marshmallows or candy-coated chocolate-covered peanuts.

Roly Poly PB-Chocolate Balls

Start to Finish: 50 minutes
24 balls

1 cup milk chocolate chips

2 tablespoons water

1 cup creamy or crunchy peanut butter

1/2 cup powdered sugar

1/2 cup light corn syrup

2 cups Cheerios cereal

1. Line a cookie sheet with waxed paper.

2. Place the chocolate chips and water in a 1-quart saucepan. Heat over medium heat, stirring constantly, until the mixture is smooth. Cool the chocolate while preparing the candies.

3. Place the peanut butter, powdered sugar and corn syrup in a medium bowl. Stir until well blended. Stir in the cereal until evenly coated.

4. Lightly spray your hands with cooking spray. For each candy, roll 1 tablespoon of the mixture into a 1 1/2-inch ball. Place the balls on the cookie sheet and press them slightly so the bottoms of the balls are flat (this stops them from rolling off the cookie sheet).

5. Spoon about 1 teaspoon of the cooled chocolate onto each ball. Refrigerate until firm, about 30 minutes. Store the candies in a covered container in the refrigerator.

1 Ball: Calories 140; Total Fat 8g; Sodium 85mg; Total Carbohydrate 16g (Sugars 10g); Protein 3g • **Exchanges:** 1/2 Starch, 1/2 Other Carbohydrate, 1 1/2 Fat • **Carbohydrate Choices:** 1

Sticky Fingers

To keep the candy mixture from sticking to your spoon when you spoon it out to make a ball, spray your spoon with cooking spray.

Color Change

Some octopuses turn white when they are scared and red when they are mad.

Ollie Octopus

Start to Finish: 1 hour
1 octopus

Glue	Cheerios cereal
3 sheets of felt (12 x 9 inch)	Clean, empty soup can
8 pipe cleaners (10 inch)	2 googly eyes
Scissors	

1. Spread glue over 1 sheet of the felt. Arrange the pipe cleaners crosswise, equally spaced, on the felt with 1 end of the pipe cleaners touching 1 long side of the felt (the pipe cleaners should hang over the other long side by about 1 inch). Spread a line of glue over each pipe cleaner. Place a sheet of felt over the first sheet, pressing down and sandwiching the pipe cleaners between the felt. Let stand until dry.

2. Cut the felt evenly between the pipe cleaners into strips. Round felt end of each strip. Glue 2 lines of the cereal onto each tentacle. Let stand until dry.

3. Bend the exposed pipe cleaner–end of each of the tentacles at a 90º angle. Tape each pipe cleaner to the sides of the can, at the bottom, making sure the tentacles are cereal-side down.

4. Glue a rectangle of felt around the can,* covering the pipe cleaner ends. Cut a 5 x 3-inch rectangle of felt to make the head. Round one end of the rectangle and glue it, rounded end up, to the can. Glue on the googly eyes. Carefully curl the tentacles.

*Safety Note:

To cover the potentially sharp top edge of the soup can neatly, cut the rectangle of felt 1/2 inch taller than needed to cover can. Glue the felt to the can matching the bottom edge of the felt to the bottom of the can. Cut the felt to the top edge at 1/2-inch intervals. Carefully spread glue inside the top edge of the can and press down each tab of felt overlapping as needed.

Frozen Yogonanas

Start to Finish: 1 hour 15 minutes
8 servings (3 coated banana pieces each)

1 to 2 containers (6 oz each) yogurt (any flavor)

3 to 4 cups Cheerios cereal

4 firm ripe medium bananas

1. Line a cookie sheet with foil.

2. Spoon the yogurt into a shallow dish. Pour the cereal into another shallow dish. Peel the bananas and cut each one into 6 pieces.

3. Roll each banana piece in the yogurt, then in the cereal to coat. Place the coated banana pieces on the cookie sheet. Freeze uncovered until firm, about 1 hour. (These are best eaten the same day they are made.)

1 Serving: Calories 130; Total Fat 1.5g; Sodium 130mg; Total Carbohydrate 28g (Sugars 11g); Protein 3g • **Exchanges:** 1 Starch, 1 Fruit • **Carbohydrate Choices:** 2

Hands On

These good-for-you treats are easier to handle (and eat) if you stick a strong plastic straw or a wooden stick with round ends in the banana pieces before you coat them with yogurt and cereal.

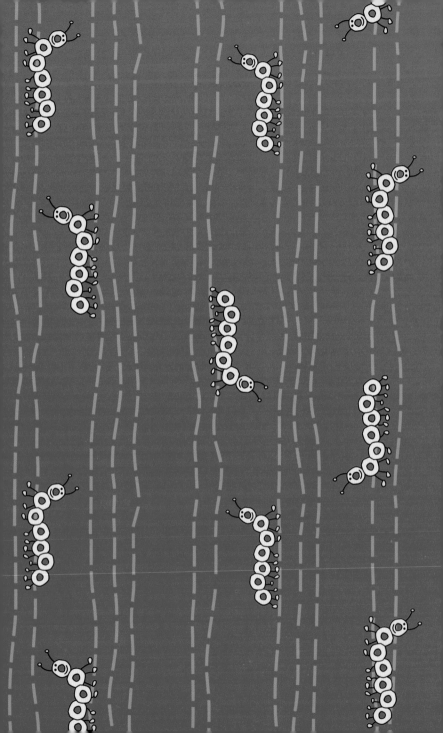

Mix 'em

Kooky Caramel Corn

Start to Finish: 1 hour 10 minutes
14 servings (1 cup each)

5 cups Multi-Grain Cheerios® cereal

8 cups plain popped popcorn

1 cup regular salted or honey-roasted peanuts

1/2 cup light corn syrup

1/4 cup honey

2 tablespoons butter or margarine

1/2 teaspoon vanilla

1. Heat the oven to 325°F. Pour the cereal, popcorn and peanuts into a large bowl. Stir to mix. Set the bowl aside.

2. Pour the corn syrup and honey into a 1-quart saucepan. Add the butter. Heat over medium heat, stirring frequently, just until the mixture starts to boil. Remove the saucepan from the heat. Stir in the vanilla.

3. Pour the syrup mixture over the cereal mixture and stir until everything is evenly coated. Pour the mixture into an ungreased 15 x 10 x 1-inch pan. With a rubber spatula, spread the mixture until it is even.

4. Bake 20 to 25 minutes, stirring once or twice, until the mixture is crispy. While the mixture is baking, place a sheet of waxed paper on the kitchen counter.

5. When the mixture is done baking, immediately pour it onto the waxed paper and spread it out into a thin layer. Cool completely, about 30 minutes. Break the caramel corn into pieces. Store in a tightly covered container.

1 Serving: Calories 210; Total Fat 10g; Sodium 140mg; Total Carbohydrate 28g (Sugars 12g); Protein 4g • **Exchanges:** 1 Starch, 1 Other Carbohydrate, 2 Fat • **Carbohydrate Choices:** 2

Go Nuts

You don't have to limit yourself to peanuts in this recipe. Try cashews, pecans, walnuts or even a mixture of different kinds.

Try using beads, buttons and dried pasta shapes as well as Cheerios cereal to create these crazy critters.

Snack Attack

Start to Finish: 10 minutes
20 servings (1/2 cup each)

2 cups Apple Cinnamon Cheerios® cereal

2 cups Cheerios cereal

2 cups Honey Nut Cheerios cereal

1 1/2 cups animal crackers

1 1/2 cups pretzel twists

1 1/2 cups cheese-fla-vored snack crackers

3 pouches (0.9 oz each) assorted chewy fruit snacks, any shape (from 9-oz box)

1. Pour all of the ingredients into a gallon-size plastic bag or 3-quart container.

2. Seal the bag and shake, or stir and cover the container.

1 Serving: Calories 100; Total Fat 2.5g; Sodium 190mg; Total Carbohydrate 19g (Sugars 6g); Protein 2g • **Exchanges:** 1 Starch, 1/2 Fat • **Carbohydrate Choices:** 1

Jungle Journey

Monkeys live in the jungle; so do tigers. Ask your child if he or she can think of other jungle animals.

Load 'n Go Gorp

Start to Finish: 30 minutes
20 servings (1/2 cup each)

1/4 cup butter or margarine

4 cups Frosted Cheerios cereal

4 cups original crispy horn-shaped corn snacks

1/2 cup raisins

1 cup miniature marshmallows

1 cup candy-coated chocolate pieces

1. Heat the oven to 300°F. Place the butter in a 13 x 9-inch pan. Place the pan in the oven for a few minutes until the butter is melted (watch so it doesn't burn).

2. Stir in the cereal, corn snacks and raisins until everything is evenly coated.

3. Bake 10 minutes, stirring every 5 minutes. Cool slightly, about 10 minutes.

4. Stir in the marshmallows and candies. Store the snack in a loosely covered container.

1 Serving: Calories 140; Total Fat 6g; Sodium 115mg; Total Carbohydrate 20g (Sugars 12g); Protein 1g • **Exchanges:** 1/2 Starch, 1 Other Carbohydrate, 1 Fat • **Carbohydrate Choices:** 1

Name Game

GORP originally stood for granola, oats, raisins and peanuts. See if your child can come up with a better name for this snack, based on its ingredients.

Something's Fishy

It's hard to tell when fish are sleeping because they have no eyelids. People who study fish are called "ichthyologists."

Go Fish

Start to Finish: 40 minutes
1 aquarium

Glue or tape	Scissors
Construction paper (any color), if desired	Cheerios cereal
	Shells and/or rocks
Large empty jar (such as a peanut butter or maraschino cherry jar)	Nylon fishing line
	Darning needle
Green pipe cleaners	Gummy candy fish
Pencil	

1. Glue construction paper to the jar lid to cover, if desired.

2. Wrap 1 pipe cleaner around the pencil. Remove the pencil. Stretch out the coils to make wavy seaweed. Cut the coiled pipe cleaner into several pieces. Bend a 1/2-inch foot onto each piece of seaweed. Cluster several weeds together at the foot and secure to the inside bottom of the jar with glue or tape.

3. Pour the cereal into the jar to a depth of about 1 inch. Arrange shells and/or rocks in the cereal.

4. Thread a length of fishing line through the darning needle. Use the needle to thread each fish onto a piece of fishing line. Hold the fish up to the bowl of the jar to determine the length of the line. Tape each line to the inside of the lid of the jar.

5. Lower the fish into the jar and screw on the lid.

Mix 'n Match Munchies

Cheerios cereal (any flavor)

Peanuts

Raisins

Animal crackers

Pretzel twists

Miniature marshmallows

Candy-coated chocolate pieces

Crispy horn-shaped corn snacks

Dried banana chips

Semisweet chocolate chips

Bite-size squares crisp wheat, corn or rice cereal

Tiny fish-shaped crackers

Plain popped popcorn

Bagel chips, broken into bite-size pieces

Oyster crackers

Diced dried fruit

1. Pour the ingredients of your choice into a plastic bag or container.

2. Seal the bag and shake, or stir and cover the container.

Mixed Bag

Package this personal, one-of-a-kind mix in a patterned tin or colorful plastic bag and give it as a gift.

Shape 'em

Cereal Cutouts

Start to Finish: 1 hour 20 minutes
16 to 20 cutouts

1/3 cup butter or margarine

1 bag (10.5 oz) miniature marshmallows (6 cups)

1/2 teaspoon food color (any color)

10 cups Cheerios cereal

Decorator icing (from 4.25-oz tube), if desired

Assorted candies or small gumdrops, if desired

1. Spray a 15 x 10 x 1-inch pan with cooking spray.

2. Place the butter and marshmallows in a 2-quart saucepan. Heat over low heat, stirring constantly, until the mixture is smooth. Remove the saucepan from the heat.

3. Stir in the food color until the mixture is evenly colored. Stir in the cereal until it is evenly coated. Pour the mixture into the pan. With the buttered back of a spoon, press the mixture in the pan until it is even. Cool completely, about 1 hour.

4. With 2-inch cookie cutters, cut the mixture into shapes. Decorate the cutouts using the decorator icing to attach the candies. Store the cutouts in a loosely covered container.

1 Cutout: Calories 200; Total Fat 5g; Sodium 210mg; Total Carbohydrate 37g (Sugars 17g); Protein 3g • **Exchanges:** 1 Starch, 1 1/2 Other Carbohydrate, 1 Fat • **Carbohydrate Choices:** 2 1/2

Creative Cutouts

The sky's the limit when it comes to crafting these cutouts. Choose hearts, stars or animals and let your child go crazy with the decorator icing. Or, skip the food color and sprinkle the cutouts with colored sugar instead.

Teddy Bear

Start to Finish: 1 hour
1 bear; 8 servings

3 tablespoons butter or margarine

3 cups miniature marshmallows

5 cups Cheerios cereal

4 large black gumdrops

2 small black gumdrops

1 roll (0.75 oz) chewy fruit snack in 3-foot roll (any flavor)

1. Place a sheet of waxed paper on the kitchen counter.

2. Place the 3 tablespoons butter and the marshmallows in a large microwavable bowl. Microwave uncovered on High for 1 to 2 minutes, stirring after each minute, until the mixture is smooth. With pot holders, remove the bowl from the microwave.

3. Stir in the cereal until it is evenly coated. Make 4 mounds of the cereal mixture on the waxed paper using 1/4 cup of mixture for each. Make another mound using 1 1/4 cups of the cereal mixture. Lightly spray your hands with cooking spray. Shape all of the mounds into balls, pressing tightly.

4. Shape the remaining cereal mixture into a cone shape, about 4 inches wide at the bottom and 6 inches tall, pressing tightly. Slightly flatten the top of the cone. Press the large ball onto the top of the cone to make the head. Press the 4 small balls to the front of the cone to make the arms and legs.

5. Slightly flatten 1 of the large gumdrops and press it onto the head to form the snout. Press 2 of the large gumdrops at the top of the head for the ears. Press the remaining large gumdrop on the back of the cone at the bottom for the tail. Press the 2 small gumdrops above the snout to make the eyes. Tie the fruit snack roll around the neck for a scarf.

1 Serving: Calories 240; Total Fat 6g; Sodium 230mg; Total Carbohydrate 46g (Sugars 23g); Protein 3g • **Exchanges:** 1 Starch, 2 Other Carbohydrate, 1 Fat • **Carbohydrate Choices:** 3

You don't have to make a boat. Try creating a page from your favorite storybook instead.

Make 'n Eat Picture

Start to Finish: 30 minutes
1 picture

1 roll (0.5 oz) yellow chewy fruit snack (from 5-oz box)	1/4 to 1/3 cup Cheerios cereal
1 roll (0.5 oz) blue chewy fruit snack (from 5-oz box)	6 to 8 raisins
Kitchen scissors	1 small paper flag, if desired
White decorator icing (from 4.25-oz tube)	1 roll (0.5 oz) red chewy fruit snack (from 5-oz box)

1. Place a sheet of waxed paper on the kitchen counter.

2. Unroll and flatten the yellow fruit snack roll. Place it on the waxed paper for the background of the picture.

3. Unroll and flatten the blue fruit snack roll. Cut it into 2 unequal pieces to look like a large wave and a small wave. Attach the large wave to the yellow background with the decorator icing.

4. Spread about 2 tablespoons of the icing into a triangle on the yellow background just above the large wave. Arrange the cereal and raisins on the icing to look like a mast and a sail. Attach the flag to the top of the mast with a dot of icing.

5. Unroll and flatten the red fruit snack roll. Cut it into the shape of a boat. Attach the boat with the icing to the large wave. Attach the small wave to the bottom of the boat with the icing.

1 Picture: Calories 360; Total Fat 8g; Sodium 230mg; Total Carbohydrate 71g (Sugars 52g); Protein 1g • **Exchanges:** 4 1/2 Other Carbohydrate, 2 Fat • **Carbohydrate Choices:** 5

Jack-o'-Lanterns

Start to Finish: 1 hour 15 minutes
12 to 15 pumpkins

3 tablespoons butter or margarine

3 cups miniature marshmallows

3 drops red food color

2 drops yellow food color

5 cups Cheerios cereal

12 to 15 whole cashews

Assorted gumdrops, raisins, candy-coated chocolate pieces, licorice

1 tube (4.25 oz) white decorator icing

1. Place a sheet of waxed paper on the kitchen counter.

2. Place the butter and marshmallows in a 2-quart saucepan. Heat over low heat, stirring constantly, until the mixture is smooth. Remove the saucepan from the heat.

3. Stir in both food colors until the mixture is an even orange color. Stir in the cereal until it is evenly coated.

4. Lightly spray your hands with cooking spray. For each pumpkin, shape about 1/3 cup of the cereal mixture into a ball. Press 1 cashew into the top center of the ball for the stem. Place the balls on the waxed paper. Cool completely, about 1 hour.

5. Attach the raisins and candies with the decorator icing to make faces on the pumpkins. Store the pumpkins in a loosely covered container.

1 Pumpkin: Calories 170; Total Fat 5g; Sodium 150mg; Total Carbohydrate 31g (Sugars 16g); Protein 2g • **Exchanges:** 1 Starch, 1 Other Carbohydrate, 1 Fat • **Carbohydrate Choices:** 2

Creating Colors

Red and yellow food color make orange. What about red and blue? Green and yellow? Remember: There's no rule saying these pumpkins have to be orange.

Holiday Balls

Start to Finish: 1 hour 30 minutes
8 balls

3 tablespoons butter or margarine

40 large marshmallows

1/2 teaspoon green food color

1/2 teaspoon vanilla

4 cups Cheerios cereal

Small gumdrops, sliced or cut into pieces

1. Place a sheet of waxed paper on the kitchen counter.

2. Place the butter and 32 of the marshmallows in a 3-quart saucepan. Heat over low heat, stirring constantly, until the mixture is smooth. Remove the saucepan from the heat.

3. Stir in the food color and vanilla until the mixture is evenly colored. Stir in the cereal until it is evenly coated.

4. Lightly spray your hands with cooking spray. For each ball, shape about 1/2 cup cereal mixture into a ball around 1 of the remaining marshmallows. Press the gumdrop pieces into the balls to decorate. Cool completely, about 1 hour. Store the balls in a loosely covered container.

1 Ball: Calories 240; Total Fat 5g; Sodium 180mg; Total Carbohydrate 47g (Sugars 26g); Protein 2g • **Exchanges:** 1 Starch, 2 Other Carbohydrate, 1 Fat • **Carbohydrate Choices:** 3

All-Season Snack

You don't have to wait for a holiday to create these yummy cereal balls. Make them whatever color you like—whenever you like.

Sweet Tweets

There are more than 9,000 different kinds of
birds in the world. How many can you name?

For-the-Birds Feeder

Start to Finish: 15 minutes
1 bird feeder

Sharpened pencil	Creamy peanut butter
Sugar ice cream cone	Cheerios cereal
Pipe cleaner (chenille stem)	Birdseed
Table knife	

1. Use the pencil to poke a hole in the pointed end of the ice cream cone.

2. Twist a knot in the end of the pipe cleaner. Thread the pipe cleaner into the ice cream cone and out the hole (the knot will hold the pipe cleaner in place).

3. Use the table knife to spread the peanut butter on the outside of the cone. Press the cereal all over the peanut butter to cover the cone. Sprinkle the birdseed over the cone, pressing it into the peanut butter with your fingers.

Christmas Trees

Start to Finish: 1 hour 45 minutes
18 trees

6 cups Honey Nut Cheerios cereal

6 tablespoons butter or margarine

4 1/2 cups miniature marshmallows

Green food color

Red cinnamon candies or sliced gumdrops

1. Line a cookie sheet with waxed paper.

2. Pour the cereal into a 4-quart bowl. Set the bowl aside.

3. Place the butter and marshmallows in a 3-quart saucepan. Heat over low heat, stirring constantly, until the mixture is smooth. Remove the saucepan from the heat.

4. Stir in the food color until the mixture is evenly colored. Pour the marshmallow mixture over the cereal and stir until the cereal is evenly coated.

5. Lightly spray your hands with cooking spray. For each tree, shape about 1/4 cup of the cereal mixture into a Christmas tree shape on the cookie sheet.

6. Press the candies into the trees to decorate. Refrigerate until firm, about 1 hour. Store the trees in a loosely covered container.

1 Tree: Calories 120; Total Fat 4.5g; Sodium 120mg; Total Carbohydrate 20g (Sugars 12g); Protein 1g • **Exchanges:** 1/2 Starch, 1/2 Other Carbohydrate, 1 Fat • **Carbohydrate Choices**: 1

Trim the Tree

These treats make great table decorations for a children's holiday party. Let each child personalize his or her tree as they please. Use decorator icing to make a garland.

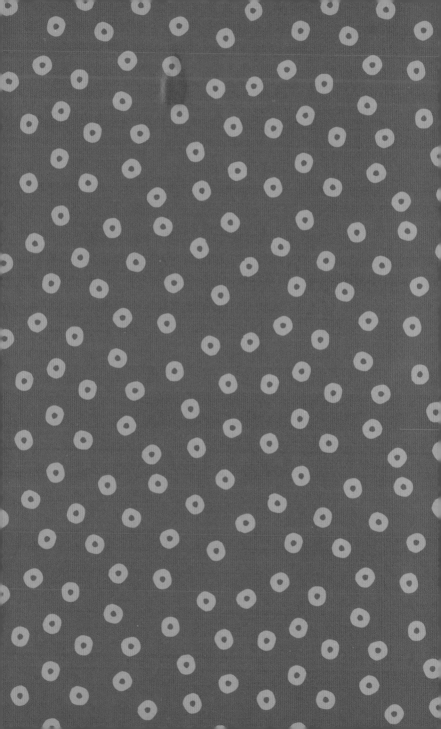

Index

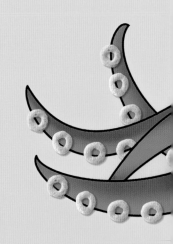